The Goddess W[...]
Through The 12-Steps

12 Rituals of Light and Love

Copyright © 2014

ISBN 978-1-62890-180-1

Created and Written by:
Amethyst Star
Baba Mecka
Shahla Coyote

Cover art from the original painting "Sige" Copyright 2000 by Pamela Matthews. Sige is one of 27 faces of the Goddess in the divination pack *"Goddesses of the New Light"*
www.grail.co.nz

Every effort has been made to locate the owner's of the artwork herein. If your artwork appears here without proper credit, or there is another issue, please contact pagan12steps@gmail.com

Forward

My chosen craft name is Shahla Coyote. The meaning behind the name Shahla is someone that wants to work with others to achieve peace and harmony, and Coyote is my animal spirit. Peace and harmony are the cornerstones of our 12-Step rituals, each one has carefully chosen elements that are specific to the step. Amethyst Star and I have been friends for many years and met Baba Mecka a few years ago at a mutual gathering place. When we discovered that we shared the gift of recovery, we each realized that something was missing, something that could make the steps more viable in our lives. We all follow the Goddess path and knew that we wanted to write rituals for each of the steps. It has been a labor of love and has allowed me to get closer to my higher power, the Spirit Goddess. I hope that this book brings you peace and harmony.

> Shahla Coyote

I came together with two other women to go through each of the steps to cement with action and ritual my growth in sobriety. My higher power includes goddesses. It seemed natural to use ritual and different goddesses to express creatively each step in recovery.

We used the Open Steps and did one step for each month. These rituals are not set in stone. If you feel that a different stone or god/goddess expresses more clearly your intention, then by all means change the ritual to be a clear expression of yourself.

Honor your sobriety by being true to what feels right to you. These rituals express an inward pull to grow in love and spirituality.

> Baba Mecka (means Grandmother Bear in Serbian)

Shahla Coyote and I, who have traveled the recovery road together for many years, met Baba Mecka for the first time a couple of years ago at an open recovery meeting. The three of us immediately began brainstorming the possibility of creating a ritual for each of the 12 Steps (modified slightly to be more goddess centered). For me each one of these rituals has been a beautiful and powerful way to express my commitment to that step. They have healed me in ways I can't even begin to describe. My journey in recovery, and along the way discovering the Goddess path, has been profound. This book has truly been a labor of light and love. I hope you enjoy it and the wonderful things that may materialize as a result of these rituals.

> Amethyst Star

Table of Contents

Step One Ritual   1

Step Two Ritual   3

Step Three Ritual   5

Step Four Ritual   7

Step Five Ritual   9

Step Six Ritual   11

Step Seven Ritual   13

Step Eight Ritual   15

Step Nine Ritual   17

Step Ten Ritual   19

Step Eleven Ritual   21

Step Twelve Ritual   23

STEP ONE RITUAL

Admitted that we have a problem and made a decision to change our lives for the better.

Begin the ceremony with a white candle in the center surrounded by one amethyst for each participant. Frankincense incense should be burning. Each participant should be given their own small white candle. Use a smudge stick to cleanse the area and participants of any negative energy.

"Let it be known that a circle is about to be cast. All who enter the Circle may do so in perfect love and perfect trust.

I call **Air** to our circle. We breathe it in with our first breaths so it is only right that it be the first element called. Come to us, Air!

Fire warms us with its passionate flame. I call Fire to our circle!

Water is a perfect balance to flame. I call Water to our circle!

Earth supports us and nurtures us. As the fourth element I call Earth to our circle.

And finally – **Spirit** is what makes us unique, what gives us courage and strength, and it is what lives on after our bodies are no more. Come to us, Spirit!"

Then light the white candle.

"One of life's paradoxes is that in order to change an unwanted situation, we must first accept it the way it is. If you wish to move forward in your life, first make peace with what you are presently experiencing. I now ask each of you to light your white candle with the flame from the center candle."

Each participant lights his/her candle as we go around the circle.

"Now repeat after me – We are protected by your might (group repeats) O Gracious Goddess, day and night (group repeats) Thrice around the circle's bound, (group repeats) Evil sink into the ground. " (group repeats)

"Now visualize a healing, white light streaming from above, into your head, and through your body. See and feel the healing energy in the flames of our candles."

"Our Spirits now join with the Goddess in celebrating our sobriety. We ask that we are given balance, clarity of mind, energy to walk our path and true compassion for others."

"**Earth**, we thank you, bless you and release you. We ask that your beauty remain with us from this ritual and be a part of our daily lives."

"**Water**, we thank you, bless you and release you. We ask that your gift of balance remain with us from this ritual and be a part of our daily lives."

"**Fire**, we thank you, bless you and release you. We ask that your passion remain with us from this ritual and be a part of our daily lives."

"**Air**, we thank you, bless you and release you. We ask that your inspiration remain with us from this ritual and be a part of our daily lives."

"**Spirit,** we thank you, bless you and release you. Please hold us close as we venture forth on our new journey."

"The circle is open but unbroken. So mote it be."

 (At the end of the ritual each participant gets an amethyst to keep as a healing stone, first step reminder)

Goddess grant me:
The power of Fire, for the energy and courage to change the things I can.
The power of Water, to accept with ease and grace what I cannot change.
The power of Air, for the ability to know the difference.
And the power of Earth, for the strength to continue my path.

STEP TWO RITUAL

Came to believe that a power greater than ourselves could, with the addition of our positive efforts, restore us to balance.

Clean the area of any negativity, burn sage in the room and smudge each person.

Begin the ceremony by lighting a white candle. In the center of the table is a caldron with myrrh and lavender, now light this incense. There is a blue and white geode on the table. This stone was cut into two pieces and I will put them together to represent that even when we are feeling broken that gentle hands can put those two halves back together. The loving hands of the goddess will balance us.

"Let it be known that a circle is about to be cast. All who enter the Circle may do so in perfect love and perfect trust."

"**Aibell**, Goddess of Air, be here tonight and share with us your inspiration. I call Air to our circle."

"**Bridgit**, Goddess of Fire, take your sacred flame and burn from us bad habits and unhealthy thinking. I call Fire to our circle!"

"**Fand**, Goddess of Water, you bring us the element of water and a balance to flame. Quench our thirst. I call Water to our circle!"

"**Isolt**, goddess of the Earth, support and nurtures us. As the fourth element I call Earth to our circle."

"**Banba**, Spirit Goddess, be with us. Spirit is what makes us part of Gaia; I honor the great web that connects us all. Come to us, spirit!"

The Circle is cast, the Goddess is with us."

"The Second Step is one of hope, faith and realization. It is a step of spiritual expression, and signifies our willingness to open our minds and our hearts to a higher power of our own understanding. In taking this step we are affirming that we BELIEVE a higher power can restore balance in our lives, so long as we make our best efforts to follow a spiritual path. "

"The Realm of Spirit is broad, roomy, ALL inclusive; NEVER exclusive or forbidding to those who EARNESTLY seek. Our actions which will lead us to our Creator, and this Higher Power will guide us in the Realm of the Spirit.

"**Isolt**, Goddess of Earth, thank you for the permanence, stability, and security you bring to our lives. We bless you and release you."

"**Fand**, Goddess of Water, thank you for your help with our goals related to emotional balance. We bless you and release you."

"**Bridgit**, Goddess of Fire, we thank you for insight in overcoming obstacles and the courage to act on their truth. We bless you and release you."

"**Aibell**, Goddess of Air, thank you for the gift of clarity...the ability to perceive what is relevant and useful. We bless you and release you."

"**Banba**, Spirit Goddess, we thank you for joining in our circle, and we ask for your blessings as you depart."

"The circle is open, but unbroken. May the peace of the Goddess go in your hearts, Merry meet, and merry part .and merry meet again. Blessed be. So mote it be."

Goddess grant me:
The power of Fire, for the energy and courage to change the things I can.
The power of Water, to accept with ease and grace what I cannot change.
The power of Air, for the ability to know the difference.
And the power of Earth, for the strength to continue my path.

Banba, Goddess of Spirit

STEP THREE RITUAL

Being responsible for our actions and honoring our connections with all life as we begin to walk on a path that is spiritual.

Burn sage and smudge each person.
Light a white candle for Spirit.
Light a light blue candle (the lighting of this candle helps us to obtain wisdom, harmony and inner light. It confers truth and guidance.)

The Labradorite Stone represents spiritual purpose as we move forward in these steps.. Each person picks a stone to keep, and passes it through the flame of the blue candle.

"Let it be known that a circle is about to be cast. All who enter the circle may do so in perfect love and perfect trust."

"**Arcangel RAPHAEL**, Guardian of Air, which is the innocence and vibrancy of the beginning of a new season. Guard us as we step forward in search of our new beginning, and restore us to reality. I call Air to our circle."

"**Arcangel MICHAEL**, Guardian of Fire, which is desire, enthusiasm, warming, and the spark of life. Guard us from false feelings of power and ego, and restore us to honesty. I call Fire to our circle."

"**Arcangel GABRIEL**, Guardian of Water, which is emotion, it feels, it dreams, it nurtures the heart. Guide us to be unselfish and loving, and restore us to peace of mind. I call Water to our circle."

"**Arcangel ARIEL**, Guardian of Earth, which is stability, it is all things that bring nourishment, fullness, and fertility. Guide us to live with integrity and truth, and restore us to balance. I call Earth to our circle."

"**Goddess Mother,** Spirit of all that is connected, we ask you to guard us and guide us as you reveal our connection, our truth, our way forward, so we may know our place in our Goddess's Universe. Come to us Spirit."

"This is a step where we move from isolation and loneliness to walking a path that includes and listens to the loving creative powers of the universe. The Feminine side is a friend giving us balance and nurturing our souls. Within this circle our spirit is safe and free to explore. Please walk with us higher power and help guide our steps. Today is Ostara, the spring equinox, as the earth blooms we listen to the goddess and see her signs of renewal."

"**Arcangel ARIEL**, Guardian of Earth, we thank you, bless you and release you. May your beauty stay with us in our daily lives.

Arcangel GABRIEL, Guardian of Water, we thank you, bless you and release you. May your balance remain with us in our daily lives.

Arcangel MICHAEL, Guardian of Fire, we thank you, bless you and release you. May your warmth remain with us in our daily lives.

Arcangel RAPHAEL, Guardian of Air, we thank you, bless you and release you. May your vibrancy remain with us in our daily lives.

"**Goddess Mother**, we bless you, thank you and release you. Please protect us and guide us going forward."

The circle is open but unbroken."

So mote it be.

Goddess grant me:
The power of Fire, for the energy and courage to change the things I can.
The power of Water, to accept with ease and grace what I cannot change.
The power of Air, for the ability to know the difference.
And the power of Earth, for the strength to continue my path.

Goddess Mother

aumega art

6

We made a searching and honest inventory of our behavior and beliefs; looking without fear at their impact on ourselves and on our relationships.

Burn sage and smudge each person.
Light a white candle for Spirit.
Light a magenta candle, (the lighting of this candle energizes rituals where immediate action and high levels of power or spiritual healing are required.)

Each participant will take a Sugilite stone. Sugilite protects, absorbs and dissolves anger, hurt, and unwanted energies. Sugilite brings spirit/light into the physical body and heart for healing, especially when placed on the Brow Chakra. This stone is perfect for healing resentments and removing negative energy. This stone brings peace of mind, well being, spiritual love and is considered androgynous. It is one of the purple stones, which help to balance right and left brain function. Used to help anyone "integrate" into the world or new surroundings (recovery).

Pass the sugilite over the magenta candle.

"Let it be known that a circle is about to be cast. All who enter the circle may do so in perfect love and perfect trust."

"**Aether**, Goddess of Air, which is the breath of life and the wisdom of our minds. Guide us as we look without fear at our lives. I call Air to our circle."

"**Hephaestus**, God of Fire, which is connected to willpower and energy. Guide us as we begin to heal our lives. I call Fire to our circle."

"**Poseidon**, God of Water, which is healing, cleansing and purification. Guide us as we look with honesty at our behaviors and beliefs. I call Water to our circle."

"**Demeter**, Goddess of Earth, giver of life, death and rebirth. Guide us as we embark on this journey of insight and discovery. I call Earth to our circle."

"**Ether,** Spirit of timelessness and spacelessness, essence of all that is within and without, we ask you to guide and direct us as we grow spiritually. Come to us Spirit."

"For the Fourth Step we need only realize that we are already spiritual; we just can't see it, due to our layers of self-structure that we have built up over it, over our lifetimes. We ask you Goddess for guidance, honesty, and thoroughness as we look within at our spiritual maladies without fear. We can then know that our real self will shine through, when we react without these desires, fears, and beliefs. To have trust in the creator, we don't have to force things, this allows for grace to happen. We can find the ground of reality, looking at our true self. We pray for guidance in each questionable situation, for sanity, and for the strength to do the right thing."

"We are unafraid of the future as we learn from our past."

"**Demeter**, Goddess of Earth, we thank you, bless you and release you. On life's journey of insight and discovery, help us be true to our purpose."

"**Poseidon**, God of Water, we thank you, bless you and release you. May your gifts of cleansing and purification open our lives to new possibilities."

"**Hephaestus**, God of Fire, we thank you, bless you and release you. May your willpower and energy give us strength in our lives."

"**Aether**, Goddess of Air, we thank you, bless you and release you. May your wisdom stay with us though out our lives."

"**Ether,** Spirit of timelessness and spacelessness, we thank you, bless you and release you. Essence of all that is within and without, we ask you to guide and direct us as we grow spiritually."

The Circle is open yet unbroken. May the blessing of the goddess stay with you. So mote it be."

Goddess grant me:
The power of Fire, for the energy and courage to change the things I can.
The power of Water, to accept with ease and grace what I cannot change.
The power of Air, for the ability to know the difference.
And the power of Earth, for the strength to continue my path.

Ether, Goddess of Spirit

www.crisvector.com

8

STEP FIVE RITUAL

We admitted to our higher power, to ourselves and to another human being what is both healthy and unhealthy in our lives. We vow to move toward a more balanced life.

Burn sage and smudge each person.

Light a white candle for Spirit.
Light a violet candle in honor of the spiritual journey we are on.
Light incense consisting of sage, rosemary and cinnamon.

"I have three Moonstones on the table: Please pick one and hold it in your hand."

Moonstone carries lunar energy and helps to balance emotional upsets. Moonstone has a gentle energy that helps to ease stress and feelings of anxiousness. It can enhance intuition. Moonstone is a good crystal tool for anyone who wishes to reflect on past circumstances to learn life lessons from those events.

"We have looked at the story that is our lives and we have reviewed our actions to gain wisdom. May the future be clear of past negativity and may we build our lives on a foundation of truth."

"Let it be known that a circle is about to be cast. All who enter the circle may do so in perfect love and perfect trust."

"**Furukara Matsuri**, Goddess of Air, be here tonight and share with us your knowledge and inspiration. I call Air to our circle."

"**Fuchi**, Goddess of Fire, take your sacred flame and burn from us bad habits and unhealthy thinking. I call Fire to our circle!"

"**Tenjin**, Goddess of Water you bring us the element of water and a balance to flame. Quench our thirst. I call Water to our circle!"

"**Yama no Shimbo**, Goddess of Earth, mother of the mountain, teach and nurture us. As the fourth element I call Earth to our circle."

"**Amaterasu Omikami** – Spirit is what makes us part of creation; I honor the energy that connects us all. Come to us, spirit!"

"The Circle is cast, the Goddess is with us."

"As we review our lives with a trusted confidante, we open our hearts and souls to the Goddess within and without. We try to hold nothing back as we honestly share our experiences and soon discover a sense of relief as the pain from a thousand hurts begins to dissipate. It is slowly replaced by a healing sense of peace and serenity. We discover that a balanced life is not only possible, it is already beginning."

"**Yama no Shimbo**, Goddess of Earth, we thank you, bless you, and release you. May the restoration of our awareness, cultivate tolerance and empathy."

"**Tenjin**, Goddess of Water, we thank you, bless you, and release you. May you cleanse our spirit as we witness the death of our past, and the transformation into our new life."

"**Fuchi** , Goddess of Fire, we thank you, bless you, and release you. May your healing warmth embrace us with the willpower needed to change our behaviors and thoughts."

"**Furukara Matsuri**, Goddess of Air, we thank you, bless you, and release you. May you continue to breathe life into us through your divine influence of truth and understanding."

"**Amaterasu Omikami**, Spirit, we thank you, bless you, and release you. As we look back into our past, we know you will protect us, and are humbled by your unconditional love."

"The circle is open yet unbroken. Take the blessings of Spirit, and the Goddesses with you each day."

So mote it be.

Goddess grant me:
The power of Fire, for the energy and courage to change the things I can.
The power of Water, to accept with ease and grace what I cannot change.
The power of Air, for the ability to know the difference.
And the power of Earth, for the strength to continue my path.

Amaterasu Omikami,
Goddess of Spirit

STEP SIX RITUAL

*We are willing to ask our higher power to help us see our path clearly,
so we may grow emotionally and spiritually.*

Burn sage and smudge each person.
Light a white candle for Spirit.
Light a blue candle for spiritual inspiration and clarity.
"I have a Lapis Lazuli stone for each person, please pick one (you may pass it over the blue candle if you want to) and hold it in your hand."
(Lapis Lazuli is a spiritual stone, it enhances enlightenment. Lapis Lazuli brings you to your highest true self).
"Step Six is the doorway to active and effective change, the goal is spiritual release. When we become willing to move in a spiritual direction we will then see how the Goddesses power is released to flow through our lives. Recovery will be a daily effort to evaluate, balance, and adjust the healthy expression of all of our Goddess-given needs."

"Let it be known that a circle is about to be cast. All who enter the circle may do so in perfect love and perfect trust."

"**Danu**, Goddesses of Air, with your knowledge and wisdom, you remind us that the power to create the life that we desire resides within us. I call Air to our circle."

"**Brigid**, Goddess of Fire, you instill in us peace, compassion and generosity, and you share with us your great gift of insight. I call Fire to our circle."

"**Matrona**, Goddess of Water, infuse us with your significant life-giving and nourishing character, as we look within for our new chosen path. I call Water to our circle."

"**Epona**, Goddess of Earth, envelope us with your grounding nature, particularly needed during these times of flux in our life. I call Earth to our circle."

"**Morrigan**, Goddess of Spirit, you bring us to the awareness of deeper layers of vision and intuition, as we go through this sometimes painful transformation. I call Spirit to our circle."

"I open myself to the beauty that is within and the beauty that is in nature. Nothing is a mistake I just have to see this creation through the eyes of love. Only through the power of love will the darkness of confusion be removed. As I breathe in and out, may this life energy remove all obstacles to my true path so my soul will be enlightened and at peace.

"**Epona**, Goddess of Earth, thank you for keeping us grounded, we bless you anfd release you."

"**Matrona**, Goddess of Water, thank you for your inspiration as we follow our new chosen path, we bless you and release you."

"**Brigid**, Goddess of Fire, thank you for your peace, compassion and generosity, we bless you and release you."

"**Danu**, Goddesses of Air, thank you for your knowledge and wisdom, we bless you and release you."

"**Morrigan**, Goddess of Spirit, thank you for the awareness of deeper layers of vision and intuition, we bless you and release you."

"The circle is open yet unbroken. Take the blessings of Spirit, and the Goddesses with you each day. "

So mote it be.

Goddess grant me:
The power of Fire, for the energy and courage to change the things I can.
The power of Water, to accept with ease and grace what I cannot change.
The power of Air, for the ability to know the difference.
And the power of Earth, for the strength to continue my path.

Morrigan
Goddess of Spirit

www.deviantart.com

STEP SEVEN RITUAL

We welcome joy, love and peace in our lives as we let go of thoughts and behaviors that hurt us.

Burn sage and smudge each person.

Light a white candle for Spirit.
Light a yellow candle to represent The Sun (sunlight of the spirit), and for Breaking Mental Blocks, Confidence, Happiness, Joy, Abundance, Money, and Health.
Have a Purple Agate stone for each person. Agates are grounding stones and one of the oldest good luck stones. They help obtain a better physical/emotional balance. They work to raise consciousness and build self-confidence. This is a stone of meditation and spiritual transformation. This stone works on the upper Chakra. It assists in allowing trust with your own intuition and opens the spiritual flood gates to a realm of endless possibilities. It gives us the space to "be" our spiritual selves and clears the mind for extraordinary vision and insight. Each participant takes a Purple Agate and may pass it over the flame of the yellow candle.

"The Seventh Step is one of letting go of the negative and welcoming in the positive. We begin blossoming in to the person our Goddess intended."

"Let it be known that a circle is about to be cast. All who enter the circle may do so in perfect love and perfect trust."

"**Njord**, God of Air, you bring us the creative breath of life and the broadening of our intellectual capacity. I call Air to our Circle."

"**Loki**, God of Fire, you bring us spontaneity, energy, mischief, and the determination of the Spirit. I call Fire to our Circle."

"**Homa**, Goddess of Water, you are changeable, sustaining, subtle and show us the infinite realm of possibilities. I call Water to our Circle."

"**Breid**, Goddess of Earth, you are supportive, reliable and keep us grounded. I call Earth to our Circle."

"**Hela**, Goddess of the Spirit, you bind all of these qualities together and give us the willingness to let go of the old and usher in the new. "

"Step Seven is a gradual healing and spiritual process once we become willing to feel instead of resist. Our primary task is acceptance and self- love. From that place, all good things will happen and come to us. Step Seven gives us permission to come as we are and bring our needs and desires to our Higher Power."

"The most healing gift of all is self-acceptance, an immediate, ever-present acceptance of self, of all we are and have been, and of all we have been through. The more we can accept ourselves, the more we will naturally evolve into who we are destined to become."

"**Breid**, Goddess of Earth, help keep us grounded as we face our daily lives. We bless you and release you. "

"**Homa**, Goddess of Water, thank you for your gift of seeing the infinite realm of possibilities. We bless you and release you. "

"**Loki**, God of Fire, thank you for your energy and determination of Spirit. We bless you and release you."

"**Njord**, God of Air, thank you for your knowledge and wisdom, we bless you and release you."

"**Hela**, Goddess of the Spirit, as you bind all of these qualities together, give us the willingness to let go of the old and usher in the new. We bless you and release you. "

The circle is now open but unbroken. So mote it be.

Goddess grant me:
The power of Fire, for the energy and courage to change the things I can.
The power of Water, to accept with ease and grace what I cannot change.
The power of Air, for the ability to know the difference.
And the power of Earth, for the strength to continue my path.

Hela, Goddess of Spirit

We make a list of all beings we have harmed, including ourselves, and we become willing to make amends to them all.

Burn sage and smudge each person.
Light a white candle for Spirit; light a black candle for removing negative influences and absorbing negativity. Light a blue candle for healing and peace.
Light some frankincense for courage.

"I have a blue calcite stone for each person. Blue calcite is a great aid to communication. Blue Calcite gives a sense of silence and calmness with an allowance to let things happen in their own time. In addition to these traits, Blue Calcite can be used to assist with tact and diplomacy."

"Please choose a stone and if you want, pass it over the blue candle. As you pass the stone over the flame, ask your higher power to bring healing and peace to you."

"It is time to live in the present and see the past for what it is and move on. Living each day and each moment we have gratitude for the simple joys in life. Step Eight is for you. You have made positive and not so positive choices. In this moment, we can begin to make amends to ourselves and those we hurt."

"Let it be known that a circle is about to be cast. All those that enter the circle can do so in perfect love and in perfect trust."

"**Nut**: Goddess of Air, bring us health and well being, so we are strong in our purpose. I call Air to our circle."

"**Selket**: Goddess of Fire, burn from us the poison that clouds our mind and give us clear and honest thinking. Let us see the truth and reality of our situation. I call Fire to our circle."

"**Anuket**: Goddess of Water, wash from us negative thoughts and fill us with your life giving energy. Let me embrace the cycles of life. I call Water to our circle."

"**Seshat**: Goddess of Earth, You are the architect and keeper of records. Give us a strong foundation and allow us to be unafraid of our past. I call Earth to our circle."

"**Isis**: Goddess of Spirit, bring to us the true magic that is life and let us enjoy our days. I call Spirit to our circle."

"Goddess, we thank you for granting us the willingness to make amends to all those we have harmed. During our travails we have caused distress to many people and we are now ready to take responsibility for our actions. The response of the person we are making our amends to doesn't matter, all that matters is we are completely willing to apologize. We know there are no guarantees that our amends will be accepted and we will accept the outcome no matter what it is. In our hearts we will know that our side of the street is clean."

"**Seshat**: Goddess of Earth, thank you for the strength, and compassion you help instill in us to forgive ourselves. We bless you and release you."

"**Anuket**: Goddess of Water, thank you for peace of mind, so we may lay our heads at night without fear of what tomorrow may bring. We bless you and release you."

"**Selket**: Goddess of Fire, thank you for clarity of a new path set before us, that we may go forth willingly to set things right. We bless you and release you."

"**Nut**: Goddess of Air, thank you for breathing life into us again so that we can continue to move forward. We bless you and release you."

"**Isis**: Goddess of Spirit, thank you for opening our hearts, and our eyes to a new way of feeling, and seeing. We bless you and release you."

The circle is now open, but unbroken. So mote it be.

Goddess grant me:
The power of Fire, for the energy and courage to change the things I can.
The power of Water, to accept with ease and grace what I cannot change.
The power of Air, for the ability to know the difference.
And the power of Earth, for the strength to continue my path.

Isis, Goddess of Spirit

www.bigbeautifullatingoddess.com

16

STEP NINE RITUAL

We make direct amends to others wherever possible and we continue positive inner and outer actions so the amends we need to make decrease.

Burn sage and smudge each person.

Light a white candle for Spirit:

Light a gray candle. This candle is a perfect balance of black and white, and therefore absorbs and repels. It draws in the undesirable energies and then sends them out to the universe for dispersal as neither a destructive nor constructive property.

"I have an Amazonite Stone for each person. It helps to eliminate worries and fears so we may communicate from the heart, and break through our boundaries. It brings clarity of thought, so we can deal with chaos and find a place of centered harmony."

"Please choose a stone and if you want, pass it over the gray candle.

Step Nine is not to win the admiration of others, but to restore our self-esteem, and further our spiritual growth. We try to bring goodness where previously we had brought discord and destruction. It takes insight, courage and dedication to make such amends, but now we have the help of our Goddess to know what to do and how to do it.

"Let it be known that a circle is about to be cast. All who enter the circle may do so in perfect love and perfect trust."

"**Cardea**, Goddess of Air, giver of new life and new possibilities. You have the power to open what is shut, and shut what is open. Help us to deal with the past so we may move forward in our future. I call Air to our Circle."

"**Vesta**, Goddess of Fire, you instill in us the willingness to get to the heart of the matter, so that we can stop looking over our shoulders for fear of our past. I call Fire to our Circle."

"**Neptune**, God of Water, you ebb and flow, you give and receive. Guide us in the same direction to humbly bend when needed. I call Water to our Circle."

"**Terra**, Goddess of Earth, goddess of morality, let us feel the remorse for our past deeds and give us the courage to set things right. I call Earth to our Circle."

"**Psyche**, Goddess of the Spirit, you exemplify the search for authentic personal growth, a reminder that the integration of our experiences, however sad or frightening they may be, matures and transforms us. I call Spirit to or Circle."

"Whenever I feel an amend is needed, I will make an amend. If it doesn't feel right, then I need to smooth the way if possible. Keeping my side of the street clean is my job. By living a clean and sober life, I am making a living amends. If I am not sure of what action I should take, I will speak to my sponsor."

"**Terra**, Goddess of Earth, we thank you for courage. We bless you and release you."

"**Neptune**, God of Water, we thank you for our humility. We bless you and release you."

"**Vesta**, Goddess of Fire, we thank you for granting us willingness. We bless you and release you."

"**Cardea**, Goddess of Air, we thank you for the new possibilities you have opened up to us. We bless you and release you. "

"**Psyche**, Goddess of the Spirit, thank you for giving us the opportunity for personal growth. We bless you and release you."

"The circle is open yet unbroken. Take the blessings of Spirit, and the Goddesses with you each day. So mote it be."

Goddess grant me:
The power of Fire, for the energy and courage to change the things I can.
The power of Water, to accept with ease and grace what I cannot change.
The power of Air, for the ability to know the difference.
And the power of Earth, for the strength to continue my path.

Psyche, Goddess of Spirit

18

STEP TEN RITUAL

We promptly acknowledge both our mistakes and our achievements.
We continue to take our personal inventory so we can live in peace.

Burn sage and smudge each person.

Light a white candle as it is the balance of all colors. Used for Spiritual Enlightenment, cleansing, healing and truth-seeking. Also repels negative energy and brings peace.
I have an Emerald for each person. Emerald promotes self-knowledge and helps to achieve balance and peace.

"Please choose a stone and, if you want, pass it over the white candle. As you pass the stone over the flame, ask your higher power to bring enlightenment to you."

"This step is one of the most important steps for spiritual and emotional balance. We choose a time where we can review our recent actions, reactions, and behaviors. We assess our successes and failures and ask the Goddess for guidance."

"To help us with this step I call the Mayan Bacab's to our circle."

"Let it be known that a circle is about to be cast. All who enter the circle can do so in perfect love and perfect trust."

"I call **Kan**, God of Air to our circle. Air brings us fresh insight and personal knowledge."

"I call **Cauac**, God of Fire to our circle. Fire brings us energy, courage and determination."

"I call **Ix**, Goddess of Water to our circle. Water brings us peace and grace."

"I call **Mulac**, Goddess of Earth to our circle. Earth brings us strength and balance."

"I call **Hunab Ku**, the Spirit God to our circle. Spirit connects us to all of creation. "

"When we get to this step, we have entered the world of the Spirit. Step 10 helps to keep the spiritual house clean. Our next function is to grow in understanding and effectiveness. It is as much a benefit to the one admitting the wrong as it is to the person who was wronged."

"Our new and true inner voice directs our every step on our march towards everlasting joy, peace of mind, and personal freedom. We start to become more secure in our recovery, and we start to appreciate the foundation that we've built. Righteous living, integrity, honesty, and positive motivation become a way of life."

"We are glad that our spiritual house is clean so our life can be more joyous."

"**Mulac**, Goddess of Earth, we thank you, bless you and release you. May your strength and balance stay with us."

"**Ix**, Goddess of Water, we thank you, bless you and release you. May your guidance bring us peace and grace. "

"**Cauac**, God of Fire, we thank you, bless you and release you. May your blessing of energy, courage and determination stay with us."

"**Kan**, God of Air, we thank you, bless you and release you. May the insight and personal knowledge you have given remain with us."

"**Hunab Ku**, we thank you, bless you and release you. May your Spirit connect us to all of creation. "

"**Mayan Bacab**, we thank you bless you and release you. Thank you for your help.
"The circle is open yet unbroken. Take the blessings of Spirit, and the Goddesses with you each day. "

"So mote it be."

"The circle is open yet unbroken. Take the blessings of Spirit, and the Goddesses with you each day. So mote it be."

Goddess grant me:
The power of Fire, for the energy and courage to change the things I can.
The power of Water, to accept with ease and grace what I cannot change.
The power of Air, for the ability to know the difference.
And the power of Earth, for the strength to continue my path.

Spirit Hunab Ku

STEP ELEVEN RITUAL

Through our meditations and actions we seek continued inner growth and contact with our higher power.

Burn sage and smudge each person. Take some frankincense, licorice and spearmint herbs and burn on some charcoal.

Light a purple candle as it helps brings one closer to the divine and strengthens spirituality. Purple can assist in meditation.

"I have a Kunzite stone for each person. Please choose your stone. Kunzite is an extremely spiritual stone with a high vibration. It radiates peace and connects one to universal love. It shields your aura and can help induce a deep meditative state. This stone can activate your heart chakra and aligns it to your third eye and your throat."

"To help us with this step, I call **Durga** to our circle to battle all destructive forces in our lives."

"I call **Tara**, Goddess of Air into our circle. May her spirit blow into us. I call Air to our circle."

"I call **Kali**, Goddess of Fire, may her power burn away thought patterns that are no longer needed. I call Fire to our circle."

"I call **Ganga**, Goddess of Water, to our circle. Water washes away debris and cleans our thoughts. I call Water to our circle."

"I call **Sita**, Goddess of Earth to our circle. Earth gives us a foundation of balance and strength. I call Earth to our Circle"

"I call **Lakshmi**, the Goddess of Spirit and divine wisdom to our circle."

"Step Eleven represents our principal means of communication with our Higher Power. As we grow in this program, we become more and more dependent on this form of communication as the way to spiritual balance. Through meditation we feel a stronger connection to our higher power and a sense of belonging within the universe. We may get a glimpse of our higher purpose and a sense that all will be well. We know that our higher power watches over us with love and light."

"**Sita**, Goddess of Earth, we thank you for instilling in us, loyalty and dedication. We bless you and release you."

"**Ganga**, Goddess of Water, we thank you for good fortune and washing away sins of the past. We bless you and release you."

"**Kali**, Goddess of Fire, you represent the past, present, and future. Thank you for being a guiding light on our new path. We bless you and release you."

"**Tara**, Goddess of Air, we thank you for helping us overcome obstacles, and alerting us to physical and spiritual danger. We bless you and release you."

"**Lakshmi**, Goddess of the Spirit, thank you for giving us material and spiritual wealth, and prosperity. We bless you and release you."

"The circle is open yet unbroken. Take the blessings of Spirit, and the Goddesses with you each day.   So mote it be."

Goddess grant me:
The power of Fire, for the energy and courage to change the things I can.
The power of Water, to accept with ease and grace what I cannot change.
The power of Air, for the ability to know the difference.
And the power of Earth, for the strength to continue my path.

Lakshmi, Goddess of Spirit

www.amritsartemples.in

STEP TWELVE RITUAL

Having had a spiritual awakening, we offer to help others along the path and we practice these principles in all our affairs

Burn sage and smudge each person.

Light sandalwood incense. Sandalwood helps us with our Spirituality, and Communication of Prayers.

Light a white candle for Spirit:

"I have a Charoite stone for each person. This stone represents spiritual transformation, and inspires service to the light and to others. Please choose a stone and if you want, pass it over the Spirit candle."

"In reaching step twelve, we have asked the help of many Gods and Goddesses. We are transformed beings on a spiritual path, and now we must be willing to give it back as it was given to us. We must move forward from this day and treat others how we want to be treated, reach our hands forward to the still suffering, while serving the Goddess as best we can."

"Let it be known that a circle is about to be cast. All who enter the circle may do so in perfect love and perfect trust."

"**Yakshi**, Goddess of Air, help us to stay grateful for each breath we take. I call Air to our Circle."

"**Agni**, God of Fire, you are the spark of life, burn into us that same desire to stay useful to the Goddess. I call Fire to our Circle."

"**Ganga**, Goddess of Water, bestow upon us your heavenly blessings, so that we may be open to all who ask for our help. I call Water to our Circle."

"**Bhumi**, Goddess of Earth, You teach us to live in harmony, to respect all living creatures. I call Earth to our Circle."

"**Aditi**, Goddess of the Spirit, mother of all the Gods and Goddesses, you are the guiding light on our spiritual path. I call Spirit to or Circle."

"This step begins with the love and lessons we have had in the previous steps and the gift it promises of a spiritual awakening. As we learn to become more aware we naturally want to share it with others."

"**Bhumi**, Goddess of Earth, we bless you, thank you and release you."

"**Ganga**, Goddess of Water, we bless you, thank you and release you."

"**Agni**, God of Fire, we bless you, thank you and release you."

"**Yakshi**, Goddess of Air, we bless you, thank you and release you."

"**Aditi**, Goddess of the Spirit, mother of all the Gods and Goddesses, we bless you, thank you and release you."

"The circle is open yet unbroken. Take the blessings of Spirit, and the Goddesses with you each day. "

So mote it be

Goddess grant me:
The power of Fire, for the energy and courage to change the things I can.
The power of Water, to accept with ease and grace what I cannot change.
The power of Air, for the ability to know the difference.
And the power of Earth, for the strength to continue my path.

Spirit Goddess Aditi

www.hinduofuniverse.com

Made in the USA
Las Vegas, NV
08 November 2023

80476310R00021